BookRags Literature Study Guide

Miracle At Philadelphia by Catherine Drinker Bowen

Copyright Information

ISBN: 978-1-304-55665-3

Table of Contents

Plot Summary

Miracle at Philadelphia is Catherine Drinker Bowen's narrative account of the Constitutional Convention that is held in 1787, during which delegates from 12 of the 13 newly independent American states hammer out what will become the United States Constitution, which is still in effect today. Bowen works from the diaries and notes of delegates, including James Madison, and includes contemporary newspaper accounts to paint a human portrait of the Convention, complete with the tensions and dissensions between states that threaten to tear apart the Convention and perhaps even the young country.

Bowen focuses on a very specific slice of American history in her book, condensing nearly five months of almost continuous meetings into approximately 300 pages. The Constitutional Convention, although it was not called this at the time, takes place during one of the hottest Philadelphia summers that the local residents can remember. Bowen uses the worsening heat to add a sense of weariness or even delirium to the proceedings as the delegates consider and reconsider motion after motion.

Bowen begins by providing a short description of the events leading up to the Convention. In 1787, the states are connected through the Articles of Confederation, which were adopted during the Revolutionary War with England. These articles provide for a Congress with representatives from all the states. The Congress is in session in New York as the Convention opens.

The Articles of Confederation have been found to be ineffective in some areas of government, particularly in trade. Congress calls for a convention of the 13 states to meet and propose modifications to the Articles. What the Convention produces, however, based largely on a proposal brought by the delegation from Virginia, is a completely new constitution that outlines a national government that is apart from and above the individual states.

George Washington sits as President of the Convention, which opens in

May 1787. Other well-known names from American history are also present, including Benjamin Franklin, Alexander Hamilton, James Madison and George Mason. Bowen provides brief background information on these and other prominent delegates. However, with 55 delegates attending at different times over the course of the summer, the book sometimes becomes difficult to follow.

Two-thirds of the way through the book, Bowen breaks away from the narrative of the Convention and supplies a description of the United States and its people at the time, as seen through the eyes of foreign visitors. These visitors' astonishment and amusement at the very different Americans accentuates the fact that the experiment in government that is about to be undertaken has never been tried on such a scale before.

Following this description, Bowen returns to the narrative of the Convention and focuses on some of the more contentious issues that threaten to dissolve it, such as the Western Territory, slavery, and how the states should be represented in Congress. These questions continue to be raised among the states as the new Constitution is considered for ratification. Bowen ends her narrative with the ratification of the new Constitution.

The Scene. Origins of the Convention. Summary and Analysis

Miracle at Phildelphia is Catherine Drinker Bowen's narrative account of the Constitutional Convention that is held in 1787, during which delegates from 12 of the 13 newly independent American states hammer out what will become the United States Constitution, which is still in effect today. Bowen works from the diaries and notes of delegates, including James Madison, and includes contemporary newspaper accounts to paint a human portrait of the Convention, complete with the tensions and dissensions between states that threaten to tear apart the Convention and perhaps even the young country.

Bowen begins by setting the scene and giving an overview of the convention and its more famous members. The summer of 1787 is hot and humid as 55 delegates of 12 of the 13 new United States, from every state except Rhode Island, meet in Philadelphia in the Pennsylvania State House, which is now known as Independence Hall.

The names of many of the delegates are familiar to most Americans, and include George Washington, Alexander Hamilton, Benjamin Franklin and James Madison. Franklin is an elderly man in his 80's, but most of the other delegates are in their 30's. Even so, Bowen says, they are respected as men of experience and maturity. "Men aged sooner and died earlier in those days," Bowen states. (p. 4).

They have come to address the problems faced by the states under the Articles of Confederation, the organizational document that has governed the relationships between the independent states following the Revolutionary War. The war has left the Confederation in debt. Some states have been paying their share, others have not, and tension between the states is mounting. The Articles of Confederation created a national Congress but gave it no power to collect money to pay the public debt.

In recognition of the shortcomings of the Articles, Congress has called a convention to consider revising it. Washington, Madison and

Hamilton have been the strongest voices in this movement to reform the Articles. Washington, as the former General of the Continental Army, is deeply aware of the problem of raising money among the states, having had experienced the hardships from lack of funds during the Revolutionary War. He has also witnessed first hand the strong ties that his soldiers had to their home states, even considering them as independent countries in themselves. The disorder among the states, Washington feels, can only be addressed with a unifying national government.

Hamilton was with Washington during the war, and has similar feelings that a national government is needed. As a member of Congress, he drafted a resolution to call a convention for this purpose, but the independent states did not support it. As part of a commission to examine interstate commerce, called the Annapolis Convention, Hamilton had written a report to Congress recommending that a federal convention be held with delegates from each state to address interstate commerce. Commerce is at the root of many of the rivalries between the states at the time, with many maintaining their own navies and customs laws. Problems within the states are also on the minds of the delegates. In 1786 in Massachusetts, Shay's Rebellion has taken place, where hundreds of farmers have marched on local courthouses over high taxes.

This rebellion is fresh in the memories of Congress when in 1787 they call for a convention for the "sole and express purpose of revising the Articles of Confederation." Seventy-four delegates are named, with 55 actually showing up. In New York, Congress is in session, but has difficulty maintaining a quorum with many of its members having gone to Philadelphia for the Convention. Some are skeptical that anything good will come of the Convention, guessing that Americans will not welcome any extreme changes.

The Convention begins in May, but delegates arrive sporadically over several months. Some simply do not have the funds to send their delegates right away. Rhode Island, afraid that a strong central government would require it to give up its state currency, does not send any delegates and is widely ridiculed for it by the other delegates.

Madison arrives early, well-prepared to argue in favor of a strong federal government. He has already studied and written widely on the subject, and has spelled out a plan for the Convention to propose a constitution to Congress for its approval, which will then be presented to the states for ratification. Madison, Washington and Hamilton are share the belief that this is a very serious matter, and that the time to resolve it has come.

Bowen provides a good, brief introduction to the events leading up to the convention, telling why it was thought necessary and the names of the major figures involved. The reader is drawn into the narrative through recognition of many of the names that are learned from childhood. As the account of the Convention continues, many more of the delegates will be introduced, some of who are perhaps not as familiar.

The Delegates and the State House. Washington and Madison. Summary and Analysis

General Washington arrives in Philadelphia on May 13, the day before the Convention is to open. He is given a hero's welcome and makes his way to the home of Benjamin Franklin. Franklin is now in his 80s and has reached a level of international renown as an inventor and a thinker. He is perhaps the most "prestigious" member of the Convention, Bowen suggests.

On May 14, the day the Convention is to start, only the two states of Pennsylvania and Virginia are represented. Muddy roads and long distances keep delegates away until May 25, when a quorum of seven states is reached. As they wait for their colleagues, the delegates from Virginia and Pennsylvania meet and discuss the upcoming Convention. During this time, the Virginians write up 15 "resolves" which will eventually become the foundation of the final Constitution.

Virginia is the first state to name delegates, and has sent seven of them, including Washington and Madison. Not in the delegation from Virginia is Patrick Henry, who is conspicuous in his absence, Bowen suggests. Henry had been named a delegate, but refused to attend, choosing to focus on state politics. Another notable absence among the delegates is Sam Adams from Boston, Bowen notes. Adams will become one of the most outspoken opponents of the new Constitution.

As the delegates arrive in Philadelphia, they are announced in the newspapers. There are two other large meetings taking place at the same time, a Presbyterian convention and a meeting of the Society of Cincinnati, a veteran's organization that includes Washington as its president. Washington's membership in the group is problematic for him, Bowen says, because of the fear among some that the group may gain the political strength to create an aristocratic, military class.

Washington makes the rounds of Philadelphia society and stays with John Morris, another delegate to the Convention and the wealthiest man in Pennsylvania. Morris would eventually lose his fortune and die without a penny.

With all the socializing, Bowen imagines, it is probably difficult for the delegates to maintain the secrecy the Convention adopted as a rule. The policy of secrecy is controversial, but has a precedent in the Continental Congress and the British House of Commons, both of which were closed to outsiders.

The State House, where the Convention takes place, also houses the chamber of the Pennsylvania Supreme Court and is the regular home of the state legislature, which has adjourned for the summer. The Convention meets in the 40 by 40-foot east room normally used by the legislature, and the same room where the Continental Congress met and where the Declaration of Independence was signed.

Delegates sit at tables during the meeting, with three or four per table. Delegates continue to arrive over the course of the summer, and drift in and out of the meeting during the day, so there are usually not more than 30 people in attendance at any one time, despite there eventually being 55 delegates.

Each delegate is introduced to the assembly, and the enactments of the state legislatures naming the delegates are read aloud. Some states have made short pronouncements, while others, including Virginia, have included long preambles giving specific expectations of the Convention. Virginia's preamble calls attention to the fact that the territories of England and Spain surround the new United States, and that disunity could make them vulnerable to these countries.

After the credentials are read, the delegates settle down to the business at hand. They quickly realize the relatively high expense of living in the city. State budgets are tight, and the delegates find themselves having to repeatedly ask for more money as the Convention drags on. Many of the delegates are considered wealthy men in their own right, but Bowen explains that the wealthiest of them "boasted more land than money." (p. 27)

On Friday, May 25, a sufficient number of states are represented to form a quorum, and the Convention officially opens. Washington is elected unanimously to the office of president of the Convention, and takes a seat on a raised dais. Major Jackson of South Carolina is elected the official secretary, but Bowen remarks that his essential outline of the proceedings reveals little about what takes place in the secret meetings. It is Madison, who purposefully seats himself in the center of the group to hear everything. He also takes the most detailed notes. He uses every waking hour between the sessions to write out what has occurred. His account is not published until 30 years after the Convention. Other members also take notes and write accounts, but Madison's remains the fullest and richest, Bowen states.

Bowen's narrative has moved back and forth between an overall view of the events, a chronological account, and background information that sets the stage. She will continue in this approach throughout the book, but as the Convention now begins, she begins to focus on a more chronological narrative.

In Convention. Randolph Introduces the Virginia Plan. Summary and Analysis

Bowen returns to the opening of the Convention. After Washington is elected president and gives a short address, the secretary Major Jackson reads aloud the credentials of the delegates from the nine states present. Bowen summarizes some of these credentials, which have been approved by the state legislatures. In them are found reference to the pressing problems of the states, including the differences between the agricultural South and the commercial North, the tension between the small and large states, and the control of the western territory on the frontier.

Through all the documents presented by the legislatures runs the theme of sovereignty. The independence and sovereignty of each state is explicitly mentioned in the Articles of Confederation, and many states are wary that the Convention may seek to supplant it with a national government.

On the Monday following the formal opening of the Convention, several more delegates arrive, including Benjamin Franklin, who is in poor health and is carried to the State House in a sedan chair he has brought from Paris. George Wythe of Virginia rises to deliver the report of the rules committee, which has met over the weekend. It is decided that the Convention will follow a formal parliamentary format with seven states forming a quorum and a majority of those present able to decide questions. The rules allow for questions that have been decided to be reconsidered, however, which provides flexibility. A rule that would allow a member to call for a roll call vote on any matter is struck down. Releasing members from binding votes and allowing questions to be reconsidered allowed for compromise and reason to play a large role in the formation of the Constitution, Bowen suggests.

After the rules are agreed upon, Wythe reads a letter from some leading merchants of Rhode Island. The Rhode Island legislature has voted against sending a delegation to the Convention. The letter from the merchants is in repudiation of this action, and expresses hopes for a successful conclusion to the Convention.

Following the reading of this letter, Governor Edmund Randolph of Virginia presents the 15 resolutions prepared by the Virginia delegation. These resolutions become known as the Virginia Resolves or the Virginia Plan. This plan will act as a starting point for the discussion of a new constitution, and will eventually form the basis of the constitution that is finally adopted. Randolph speaks for several hours. Following Randolph, Charles Pinckney of South Carolina presents a similar plan for a federal government. Because it is now late, no discussion is held over these plans. The assembly adjourns with a resolution to convene the next day into a committee of the whole.

Bowen introduces some of the issues that the Convention will find the most difficult to grapple with, in particular the notion of a strong central government that is superior to the state legislatures. The Virginia Plan, which suggests that such a government is necessary to prevent the Confederation from tearing itself to pieces, is controversial. Bowen will examine some of the controversy and the subtle differences between a federal and national system in the next chapter.

Federal versus National. The Two Supremes. The City of Philadelphia. Summary and Analysis

Bowen explains the procedure of going into a Committee of the Whole. This practice, which is often used by the British House of Commons, allows an assembly to discuss and vote on issues without taking formal action.

On May 30, Randolph presents an amended version of the first three Virginia Resolves. He proposes a three-part "national government, consisting of a supreme legislative, executive and judicial." (p.41) It is a drastic proposal, and provokes extensive discussion. Elbridge Gerry of Massachusetts suggests instead a federal government of three parts. The difference between the two will take up much of the discussion for the next several days. The present form of government is based on the idea that the states are a federation of independent entities, and the federal model of government simply facilitates agreements between the states but is not superior to them. A national government, such as Randolph proposes, would be superior to the state governments.

Governor Morris of Philadelphia rises to speak in favor of the supreme national government. The states would retain their powers, he suggests, only having to yield in matters where they clash with the national government. There cannot be "two supremes" he says. A confederation of states with a federal government will not last, he suggests, and will end in despotism.

This is a strange concept to the delegates, Bowen suggests, as a national government that is responsible directly to the people is like nothing any country has currently. James Wilson of Pennsylvania sums up the matter by asking whether a government should be over people or over states. He argues that individuals are the objects of government, and so a national government is necessary.

The assembly turns to the practical question of how a national legislature would be elected. These are addressed by the fourth and fifth Virginia Resolves. This practical approach to matters was to be common to the debate, Bowen suggests. The men of the assembly are for the most part experienced in government and use little time in the discussion of theory, but quickly turn to the practical question of how a process would work.

The practical question is how to balance the election of the legislature with the common fear that opening the vote to the people will result in mob rule. The recent rebellion in Massachusetts is on the minds of some as they suggest that the state legislatures should elect senators, not the common people. Gerry warns of the danger of "the excess of democracy." (p. 45)

Others do not share the view that rebellion is a bad thing. Writing from Paris, Jefferson is dismissive of the importance of Shay's rebellion, and considers that a certain level of anti-government spirit is desirable. Delegates Benjamin Franklin and George Mason share this faith in the common people. Despite disagreement on this matter, Bowen states that it is becoming clear at this point that the proposed two houses of the legislature should not be based on class. All have a distrust of monarchy and aristocracy.

On May 31, the Committee of the Whole passes the first three Virginia resolves. Like most of the state legislatures at the time, the new national legislature will have two houses. Only Benjamin Franklin is openly opposed to this idea. Surprisingly, Bowen suggests, the fourth Virginia Resolve is also passed, that the House of Representatives will be directly elected. She suggests that in these early days of the convention, the smaller states, which stood to lose influence by direct election because of their small populations, had not yet organized in opposition. Both of these decisions will be reconsidered in later votes, Bowen says.

Part of the sixth Virginia Resolve calls for the ability of the national government to use force against a state that defies it. Madison moves to postpone a vote on this issue, which passes. This controversial proposal will not make it into the final constitution.

Bowen turns to a description of the city of Philadelphia. It extends nine blocks from the Delaware River on the east side. Most of the delegates are staying nearby with friends or in boarding houses. Between sessions, they meet, socialize, and prepare for the next day's meeting. They often drink heavily, as is the custom Bowen says. The city has a regular popular market twice a week, and museums, libraries and bookstores. There is also a seamier side, with prisoners heckling passers-by from their cells and filth in many of the streets. As Americans begin manufacturing their own goods, the city is growing. Trade with China has started a few years previously, and new products are continuously becoming available.

The Chief Executive. Wilson of Philadelphia, Dickinson of Delaware. Dr. Franklin Speaks his Mind. June 1-6. Summary and Analysis

Delegates continue to come and go, and the danger that the Convention may dissolve is a real possibility, Bowen writes. On Friday, June 1, the Committee of the Whole considers the seventh of the Virginia Resolves, that a national executive be instated.

James Wilson of Pennsylvania rises to suggest that the national executive be a single person. This worries some members, who imagine the autocratic colonial governors or a monarch. Wilson argues that the executive portion of the government must be "vigorous," and that this trait can best be found in an individual.

Wilson is opposed by some who compare the idea to the British System. Bowen suggests that this comparison comes naturally, as all the delegates were born under British rule. The comparisons to the government of England, both favorable and otherwise, will continue throughout the Convention, although many will find them troubling.

John Dickenson speaks in support of a single executive. He is already well known as an author, as Bowen describes him, and is one of the strongest voices for a national government. Randolph, in turn, proposes a three-member executive system intended to spread out the influence geographically. Pierce Butler of South Carolina objects, referring to a similar system in Holland. It is feared that a hereditary monarchy may evolve from it.

The topic turns to the question of the veto, called the "executive negative." Benjamin Franklin speaks out against an executive veto, saying he has seen the power abused by the former governor of Pennsylvania to extort money from the legislature. Franklin is opposed to any compensation for the executive, reflecting his Quaker ideals that it is more honorable to serve without pay.

As the debate over a single or multiple executive branch proceeds,

Bowen writes that Washington sits quietly with the other Virginia delegates. It is assumed that whatever the final form of government, Washington will somehow be at the head of it. Later, Madison writes that the debate is embarrassing. Franklin moves that executive position be unpaid and Hamilton seconds it. The question is postponed, however the Committee votes 7-3 that there should be just one executive.

Virginia Resolve number eight is now taken up. This resolve proposes that the judicial and executive branches should join to review new laws. There is opposition to this. Although many of the men are lawyers and judges, Bowen says, they are also aware of the widespread prejudice against those of that profession. Giving them too prominent a role in the final government might endanger the chances of gaining approval from the states.

Coming around again to the issue of the executive veto, the Committee votes 10-0 against it. Madison suggests that Congress might be given the power to override an executive veto. This is not discussed at this time, but the idea will eventually be included in the final Constitution.

The ninth resolve is now considered, which covers the appointment of judges. The resolve proposes that federal judges who will sit in the states be appointed by the state legislatures. The question is postponed.

On Tuesday, June 5, the remaining Virginia Resolves are considered. Resolve 10, concerning the admission of new states, is affirmed. Resolve 12 states that the current Congress should remain in place until any new form of government is implemented. It is also passed. The Committee postpones decisions on the 11th, 13th and 14th Resolves, which cover a guarantee of a republican government to the states, amendments to the constitution, and the requirement of state officers to take an oath to support the national government.

The 15th Resolve provokes an interesting debate. It concerns ratification of whatever document is produced by the Convention. Some feel a popular vote should be taken. Others propose that special conventions be held to consider ratification. The question is postponed.

As the subject changes frequently and questions are considered and reconsidered, Bowen is faced with the problem of keeping the narrative coherent and easy to follow. As will be described in later chapters, the Convention will drag at times as delegates give long speeches and the summer heat wears on. Bowen attempts to break up the monotony by inserting biographical and background information, which sometimes interrupts the flow of the proceedings.

Life, Liberty and Property. The People at Large. The Method of Electing Congressmen. June 6-7. Summary and Analysis

On June 6, the Committee returns to the fourth Resolve, which proposes that the House of Representatives should be directly elected by the people. It is recognized that it will be important for the people of the country to feel connected to the new government for it to be successful, yet there is a real fear among the delegates that "indigent" people might end up being elected to office without some kind of mitigation.

Bowen inserts a segment about the importance of property in the new country. Ownership of property is equated with freedom. Even those without property are able at this time in history to work hard enough to obtain a plot of land. Even so, there are of course more and less wealthy people. The delegates are for the most part more propertied than the common people. This wealthier class differs in how they view the common people and their role in government. Men like Elbridge Gerry, remembering Shay's Rebellion, see them as something that government should be protected from. Jefferson, on the other hand, views them more idealistically as the healthy basis of the republic.

Many states require that a person own property in order to vote, and have minimum property requirements to hold office. The final Constitution will not make any requirements for holding national office, and will leave the question to the states to decide for themselves.

The delegates continue to discuss the question of popular election. Madison is firm in his belief that at least one house of the legislature be directly elected by the people.

George Read of Delaware makes the surprising proposal that the state governments should be done away with and replaced by a national government. Given that Read represents on of the smallest states, this suggestion seems even more startling. Bowen interjects that the country is largely rural at this time, and to some holding a popular election seems impractical. The vote is 8-2 against popular election of the House of Representatives.

The following day, the fifth Resolve is reconsidered, concerning the Senate. Gerry, mainly concerned with commercial interests, favors the election of the Senate by the state legislatures. Bowen describes Gerry as being shortsighted in his bias toward commercialism, although it is easier to make this assessment looking back from this side of history. It seems likely that most of the delegates, being relatively wealthy men, were balancing their financial concerns with their sense of duty toward the new country.

John Dickenson supports Gerry's idea, using an image of the solar system with the national government as the sun and the states as planets to illustrate his concept of the role of the states in the national government. James Wilson opposes the idea, and proposes popular election. On Dickenson's motion, the delegates vote that the Senate should be elected by the state legislatures. This proposal will eventually make it into the final Constitution.

The Congressional Veto. Proportional Representation. The Delegates Write Home. Summary and Analysis

On June 8, the delegates take up the congressional veto question once more. Wilson speaks persuasively in favor of the idea, Dickenson agrees. Gunning Bedford opposes it. It would allow larger states to "crush" smaller states and is impractical, he states. The proposal is defeated 7-4. It is interesting to note that two men who were opponents on one issue, Gerry and Dickenson, are here allies. Bowen's suggests early on that the Convention's adoption of a rule allowing questions to be reconsidered, while creating much more discussion and potential for disagreement, also provided the delegates the flexibility to change their own minds. This alignment and realignment of the delegates will contribute to the divisiveness that will appear as the Convention proceeds.

The following day, the fourth resolve is considered further with the question of how the states will be represented in the legislature. It will become a very contentious issue. Judge Brearly of New Jersey is against proportional representation, saying that it will render the smaller states powerless. He makes the drastic suggestion that the state boundaries be erased, and the country be divided into 13 equal parts. This is widely opposed for being so extreme, and possibly against the purpose for which the Convention has been called.

Paterson of New Jersey warns that his state will never support proportional representation. The issue remains divided between large and small states. Bowen wonders that this contention does not destroy the meeting entirely. She states that it is now clear to the delegates that Convention will stretch on for some time. Washington writes home for an umbrella and warmer coat, looking ahead to the fall. Bowen remarks that Washington does not seem to feel the moment is as momentous as some others do.

America Divided. Sherman's Compromise. The Committee of the Whole Makes its Report. June 11-13. Summary and Analysis

Bowen opens with a discussion of the temperamental differences between northerners and southerners, and the difference in their interests. The North-South split is one of the ways in which the Convention can be cut. The division between the large and small states is also growing.

Roger Sherman rises to again address the question of representation of the states in Congress. He proposes that the House be apportioned based on state population of free men, but that in the Senate each state have one vote. The idea is not supported, although it will be the path that is eventually followed.

Another proposal is made by Rutledge that the states be represented in the house according to how much they collect in taxes and contribute to the national treasury. This brings up the question of slavery, since slaves are considered property that can be taxed, but are also people who might be counted toward a state's population. Wilson proposes the three-fifths rule that will eventually be included in the Constitution, which states that the slave population will count at a rate of three-fifths toward determining state population and representation in Congress. On the issue of population, Franklin says that since he believes smaller states are easier to govern than larger ones he would be willing as President of Pennsylvania to give portions of his state to neighboring states to even out the population.

At the close of the day, the Committee votes on Sherman's idea to give each state equal representation in the Senate. It does not pass, but the vote is 6-5. By the same margin, it is decided that representation in both houses will be proportional to population.

Bowen fills out the setting of the Convention some more by describing the very hot, humid summer of Philadelphia. Mosquitoes, flies and bedbugs are everywhere. Decorum calls for gentlemen such as the delegates to wear woolen suits. They endure.

The secrecy rule is strongly enforced, and Bowen relates a story of Washington openly upbraiding the delegates after a stray piece of paper with one of the delegate's notes is found left behind on the floor of the State House.

The next question considered is the length of the term for representatives in the House. Proposals for one, two and three years are heard. The Committee votes for 3-year terms. The subject of payment arises, and from where the money should come. Should the states pay their own representatives, or should the national government pay them? The vote is 8-3 to pay them from the national treasury. The term of senators is discussed, but no decision is made. It is generally believed that the Senate should provide stability to the government. Gerry proposes that the Senate not be allowed to generate "money bills." This is voted down.

It is now four weeks since the Convention opened, and the Committee of the Whole is prepared to submit its report to the full Convention. Paterson of New Jersey speaks up. He asks that he be allowed to present an alternate plan to the Virginia plan. His plan is not for a national government, but a federal one. Dr. Johnson writes that it looks like a long summer ahead.

This chapter is an example of the sometimes difficult task of bringing the relatively mundane accounts of a committee meeting to life. Bowen does a good job of this, although as the delegates themselves become wearier, it is hard not to let some of that weariness creep into the writing, thus boring the reader.

The New Jersey Plan. Alexander Hamilton Makes his Speech. June 15-19. Summary and Analysis

On Friday, June 15, Paterson presents the New Jersey plan for a federal government. He claims that the Convention has been called simply to consider revisions to the current federal government, and has overstepped its authority by proposing a national government.

Supporters of the federal plan distrust strong central government. The New Jersey plan differs from the Virginia plan in some key ways. Instead of two houses in the legislature, the New Jersey plan calls for one. The Virginia plan has one executive, the New Jersey plan more than one. The New Jersey plan limits the matters on which the federal legislature can make laws. The Virginia plan as it stands allows the Congress to veto state laws. The New Jersey plan would permit the executive to use force to make states obey.

In defense of his plan, Paterson asserts that the national plan would be very expensive, requiring congressmen to travel a great distance every year. He believes that the people would not support such a plan.

Wilson answers Paterson's concern over the authority of the Convention to propose a new government by saying that he believes they have the power to propose anything, but not the power to implement it. Randolph makes another plea for the National plan, after which the assembly adjourns until Monday

On Monday, Alexander Hamilton speaks for six hours. Bowen provides some biographical background on Hamilton, who is young and considered very British in his manner. His intellect is widely respected. Bowen repeats the assessment of other historians who suggest that Hamilton is not always given his due in American history.

The other two delegates from New York, Lansing and Yates, who never vote the same way as he, distrust Hamilton. Only through the influence of his father-in-law has he been appointed a delegate at all. Bowen portrays Hamilton as lacking the passion for his home state that others displayed, instead being driven by a love of the Union as a whole.

Hamilton does not claim to offer a plan of his own, but stands to make his thoughts known, he says. He favors a single executive, chosen for life, who is given an absolute veto. Senators should also be chosen for life, he says. The House should be elected and the terms three years. State governors, Hamilton suggests, should be appointed by the national government. He points to England as a model. In his notes, Bowen says, Hamilton's idea of a strong executive goes even farther. He also believed that the executive should be hereditary and have absolute power. Yet he does not say so in his speech to the assembly.

What he does say is even too drastic for the delegates, some because of the strong executive, others because of the popularly elected House that Hamilton thought would balance it. Hamilton's speech takes up the entire day, and the assembly adjourns.

Nobody supports Hamilton's idea the next day, yet nobody rises in rebuttal, either. Bowen suggest that Hamilton might never have made such drastic proposals had the Convention not been held in secret. Hamilton's words will follow him, and he will eventually deny that he ever proposed a president for life.

On June 30, Hamilton will leave the Convention. Shortly afterward, the other two New York delegates will leave, as well, out of protest to the idea of a national government. Hamilton will occasionally return to the Convention, however, and is one of the eventual signers of the new Constitution.

Bowen jumps ahead in the narrative from time to time, as happens here in describing events that occur weeks and months after the day being described. This is necessary at times to put the events in context. However, it interrupts the linear flow of events. The reader must take care to follow closely.

The Great Debate. June 19-28. Summary and Analysis

On Tuesday, June 19, Madison is the first to speak. He systematically dismantles the New Jersey plan. He suggests that it would not prevent "internal state turmoils" like Shay's Rebellion, or prevent the states from issuing their own money to escape debts to other states. It would also be an expense to smaller states, which would have a more difficult time paying their representatives. After Madison's speech, Rufus King asks for a vote on which plan is preferred. The Virginia plan wins. The small states are not beaten, however, Bowen says. The question of representation will continue throughout the summer.

On June 20, the delegates meet in full convention with Washington presiding. The Convention's first action is to remove the phrase "national government" from the first Virginia resolve and replace it with "government of the United States."

Lansing of New York speaks out against the congressional veto of state laws as being too impractical. George Mason also feels that Congress is given too much power in the proposed plan. Luther Martin, who has arrived late at the Convention, gives a long-winded speech against a two-house Congress. He also opposes a national judiciary in the states, and believes that Congress should represent the states, not individuals.

Bowen suggests that the Convention skirts the contentious issue of how states will be apportioned representation in the new government by considering several of the smaller issues. They take up the matter of payment of Congress. Franklin again feels that they should not be paid at all. A property requirement for senators is considered. It is discussed whether national officials should be able to hold other positions in the government. Several members rise to speak on both sides of these issues.

Once the matter turns to the question of representation in the Senate, the discussion heats up. No conclusion is reached on the ratio of representation, however it is decided that senators should be appointed by the state legislatures, and should be at least 30 years old. A six-year term is agreed to. By a 10-1 vote, it is decided that senators should be paid, but the source of payment is determined by a close vote in favor of the national treasury rather than state funds. The property requirement is dropped, and it is decided that senators may hold state offices, but not other national positions while serving as senator. These small steps seem promising, Bowen states, but the crucial issue of how representation will work still looms.

The day grows hotter as Martin begins another long speech, quitting only after he becomes physically exhausted. He tries the patience of the other delegates, who criticize him openly for arriving late but still feeling as if he were free to carry on at such length.

Franklin speaks up to remind the assembly of the importance of asking for divine guidance. He moves that they begin each session with prayers led by a clergyman. In deference to Franklin, Sherman seconds the motion, but it is soon pointed out that there is no money to pay a chaplain. It is a crucial moment, Bowen says. Although Franklin's motion does not pass, it calms the heat.

Bowen hints here at the potentially explosive issue of representation of the states in the new government. A Congress with representation based on population will favor the large states, giving them more votes. The smaller states are understandably opposed to this. On the other hand, equal representation of the states will reduce the influence of the larger states. This critical disagreement will eventually threaten to break up the Convention as the delegates look for a solution.

The Tension Mounts. Europe and America. Summary and Analysis

The division between the states is growing worse, as the delegates grow more tired. Now meeting in Convention, the delegates are deadlocked over apportioning representation. The proposal that states have equal representation in the Senate is put forward. Madison strongly opposes this, and Wilson agrees. The small states fear that the larger ones will dominate them without equal representation. Madison's words offend Ellsworth of Connecticut, who protests openly to Washington.

Franklin urges compromise, but the arguments become more serious. Gunning Bedford of Delaware sums up the issue by addressing the delegates of the three largest states, Massachusetts, Pennsylvania and Virginia. "I do not, gentlemen, trust you," he says. (p. 131) He predicts that in order to protect themselves from larger states, smaller ones may band together or even join forces with a foreign country. This is too rash a statement for most delegates' taste.

Bowen turns to a discussion of the position of the United States in relation to Europe. It is much closer to France than to England, perhaps understandably, as France was an ally during the Revolutionary War against the British. Americans overseas report that the English seem to want nothing to do with Americans, while the French, just two years from their own revolution, have an affinity for the new country. Europe is watching the experiment in America even as monarchy is reaching its "peak" in much of Europe. (p. 135)

On July 2, the Convention considers the question of equal representation in the senate. The vote splits 5-5, with Georgia divided. A committee is appointed to address the question and make a report in three days. July 4th comes, and the delegates observe Independence Day. The local press is optimistic about the outcome of the Convention, unaware of the tension inside the State House.

On the fifth, the Convention hears the report of the committee and rejects it. The fight continues for several days. The last two delegates from New York leave in protest. One of Washington's friends remarks in a letter that Washington looks like he did at Valley Forge. Washington writes to Hamilton in New York that he "despairs" of seeing a favorable conclusion.

Bowen leaves the question open here, with the tension between the states at its highest and even the highest among them pessimistic about its outcome. She turns to a description of the United States and its territory in the next chapters, providing background for the battle between the states that leads up to the "Great Compromise" they will eventually strike.

Journey Through the American States. The Physical Scene. Summary and Analysis

Bowen breaks from the Convention and turns to a description of the United States as it is seen through contemporary foreign eyes. Several French and English visitors come to the US in the 1780s and 1790s. Many keep diaries and write letters about what they observe.

For the most part, the visitors are enamored of the new country and produce a romantic vision of it. Native Americans are celebrated by the Europeans for example, at a time when the prevailing American view is that the Indians are dangerous and should be exterminated. Other foreign views are equally out of step. Some foreign books on America are even written by people who have never been there.

Lured by the fantastic stories, some Europeans are probably very surprised at the harsh realities of life in the US once they arrive, Bowen speculates. It is noted that Americans seem to have an "unconquerable aversion to trees," (p. 146) cutting them down to clear pasture and farmland.

European travelers note the curiosity of Americans for news and their almost constant business. Portions of the new country are densely settled, like much of Europe, they observe, but there are also large areas of forest and rural land. French visitors are amused that the Americans have no concept of the manorial system common in Europe. They also remark on the high standard of living and wide mobility. This contrasts sharply with conditions in Europe at this time, where poverty is common and people live and die in the same place they are born.

This chapter and the next mark a transition in Bowen's narrative, which has focused more or less on chronological presentation of events. Following a description of the land and people of the US at the time, she completes the narrative of the Convention by focusing on the important issues that have arisen and how they are addressed.

Journey Through the American States, Continued. The People. Summary and Analysis

From the physical description of the new country, Bowen turns to the foreign view of the Americans as a people. Americans have a sense of equality that many Europeans find shocking, Bowen says. One is amazed to find a congressman riding in a public stagecoach, conversing with a workman.

The people are friendly and open, visitors note. They do not respond well to being told what to do, however. Foreigners are surprised to find retired military officers running inns and other businesses. In Europe, officers are from the noble classes. Americans all dress in similar fashion, they observe. These observations are of the Atlantic coast towns. In the interior life is rougher. There are few schools and young men of 14 are considered responsible adults.

American speech interests foreign visitors, who remark on the peculiar pronunciation of the New Englanders. Noah Webster begins writing about this new American language in 1789 and does more than anyone else to document and describe the speech of Americans.

Education already has a long tradition in America by this time, and new colleges continue to be founded, including the College of Physicians in Philadelphia. Medicine is a brutal profession compared to today, as Bowen describes it.

Advances in industry and science are in the near future for America in 1787. The cotton gin and textile machinery are about to come into use. Bridge building has made large steps, and experiments are made with steam-powered engines. Literature and fine arts have not yet come into their own, Americans preferring more useful pursuits.

American women are thought to be very pretty. All Americans are noted for their lack of social manners like those of Europe. One French writer says he believes this aspect of the American character is what allowed them to pose the revolution.

The Western Territory, the Land Companies and the Northwest Ordinance. Manasseh Cutler. Summary and Analysis

Bowen returns to the issues being considered at the Convention in this chapter, which is one of the longest in the book. The question of further expansion of the United States and how newly acquired land should be governed is one of the most central questions of the Convention.

The Western Territory extends from the Appalachian Mountains in the east to the Mississippi River in the West, and from Spanish Florida in the south to the Great Lakes in the north. Ten states will eventually be formed within this area. The British had given up defending the region from Indians while America was under its rule, and closed it to settlement. With independence, the territory is open again.

The states differ in how they view the territory and what they feel should happen with it. Bordering states claim different parts of the territory. They will all eventually cede their claims to the Union, after years of bargaining. In the meantime, outposts of settlers are threatening to form their own independent states. Where the border areas are controlled by Spain, it is worried that the Spanish may seek to take control. England is also eyeing the territory from its holdings in Canada.

Administering the Western Territory is not what the Convention is called to consider, but the territory is an important issue as they discuss whether the region is to be admitted as part of the Union under the new government, and whether it should have an equal footing with the other states.

Some are afraid any new states peopled by uncouth westerners might conflict with the more experienced eastern states. Settlers are pouring into the Western Territory, making the question more and more urgent. Land companies have wasted no time speculating on the new territory, including many companies supported or promoted by Convention delegates, including Washington and James Wilson.

On July 13, Manasseh Cutler arrives in Philadelphia. He has been in New York negotiating with Congress concerning a new land company called the Ohio Company, of which he is a founder. Bowen suggests that Cutler is an unscrupulous character who has just convinced Congress to pass the Northwest Ordinance, which opens the Western Territory to expansion by defining terms under which it will be governed. He has come to Philadelphia to attempt to make sure any new government proposed by the Convention does not interfere with his goals.

The Northwest Ordinance sets down the provisional government of the territory and describes how it will be apportioned. Slavery is prohibited. Any region gaining 60,000 in population would be admitted to the Confederacy as a state and could write its own constitution. These states would be on an equal footing with the existing states.

The Convention has already decided that the House will be apportioned with one representative for every 40,000 people in a state. With the rapidly changing balance of population as western settlement rapidly continues, this seems too few. The present states are worried they may soon be overpowered by new western states if they are given equal access to government.

Gerry moves that new western states be admitted in a way "that they should never be able to outnumber the Atlantic states." (p. 177) King seconds. Sherman gives his opinion that the western states are unlikely to ever outnumber the eastern ones. Gerry's motion goes down, 5-4. Governor Morris proposes admitting the new states based on area instead of population. He fears the westerners will eventually start a war with Spain. The wilderness is no place for a man to learn the art of politics, he believes. Later, Morris will write that he believes the new territories should have been ruled as provinces and given no representation in the national government.

Several delegates are opposed to Morris and argue in favor of western equality. Wilson reminds the delegates that England had also been afraid the American colonies were growing too fast and attempted to check them, with disastrous results for England. Madison also speaks in favor of western equality. As western populations grow, he says, any goods they produce or buy will have to pass through the East on their way to and from the sea. George Mason also speaks in favor of western equality.

It is while this issue is being discussed that Cutler arrives in town. He takes a room at the Indian Queen, a boarding house where many delegates are also staying. Very soon, he has been introduced to several delegates, whom he proceeds to entertain.

Bowen, working from Cutler's diary, says there is no entry of what he discussed with the delegates, but she imagines he must certainly have brought the conversation around to the Northwest Ordinance and his desire to for the new government to prevent the individual states from interfering with settlement and expansion led by the land companies. Cutler becomes very popular with many delegates, who invite him to call on them. He meets briefly with Franklin.

Bowen perhaps tries a little too hard to portray Cutler's influence as a lobbyist. She implies that he is something of a scoundrel, but offers no supporting evidence. By her own admission, his diary is blank on his dealings in Philadelphia. Throughout the book, however, she has focused on the human aspects of the Convention, which is perhaps why she chooses to include the character of Cutler even though she does not appear to have much solid information.

The Convention will return to the western question throughout the summer. It will become one of the main issues during the fight over ratification. Bowen suggests that the modern student of history is used to thinking of "disunion" as being a threat from the South. This earlier division between east and west might have been the first break in the new nation had the Convention not decided to recommend equality.

Later that year, a band of settlers led by Cutler's son, leaves for the Ohio River valley.

The Great Compromise. A King for America. Ten-Day Adjournment. General Washington Goes Fishing. Summary and Analysis

While Philadelphia newspapers speculate that the Convention is proceeding with unanimity, it is actually far from the case. On July 16, the Convention passes what would eventually come to be known as the Great Compromise. This promises equal representation for each state in the Senate to counter the proportional representation in the House. Bowen describes this as perhaps the most crucial decision made by the delegates, and one that nearly ends the entire Convention. Later accounts of delegates confirm that the question is extremely contentious. Washington and others will eventually point to the compromise, which emboldens the smaller states at the Convention, as a turning point.

The New Hampshire delegates finally arrive at this time, and characterize the argument of the most "vigorous minds" as advocating for a "high-toned monarchy." (p. 188) Bowen finds it curious that the idea of a monarch seems to be so naturally appealing to the young, sharp thinking men like Hamilton. Yet many do seem to welcome the idea. Some, like George Mason, even expect that a monarch will eventually arise under the new government. Bowen notes that the first Congress held under the new Constitution paused in celebration of the birthday of George III.

The Convention considers and reconsiders the method of electing the president, some wanting the position appointed by Congress, others for a popular election. The question arises of whether the president can be impeached, and by whom. The term of office is considered several times, and whether a president can serve more than one.

The monarch question comes to the forefront when a newspaper reports on a movement to bring the second son of George III to America to be installed as a king. The rumor begins that the Convention is considering this. The Convention responds in a Philadelphia paper that while its proceedings are secret, it will deny that they are considering installing a new monarch.

On July 26, the Convention appoints a Committee of Detail, charged with taking the various measures that have been decided and arranging them into a single report on which the entire Convention can vote. The Convention adjourns for ten days while this task is completed. Anticipation is high among the states, whose delegates cannot yet reveal the principles of the Convention's decisions.

During the adjournment, Washington rides out to the countryside with friends to go fishing. Bowen turns to a description of the man who would become the first President of the United States under the new Constitution. Working from his letters and contemporary descriptions, she remarks that opinions of his character vary widely, but that all agree he is dignified and graceful.

Washington rides with Morris to Valley Forge, where Morris fishes and Washington visits the site of his encampments where he and the American army spent a terrible winter during the Revolutionary War. Bowen imagines his sadness as he rides over the dusty fields where many soldiers died.

He returns to Philadelphia and makes another fishing excursion to Trenton. Washington is constantly noting the farms and crops he sees along the way, and asking about their cultivation. He sends this information back to his own farm in Virginia.

Committee of Detail. The Slavery Compromise. Summary and Analysis

Monday August 6, the Committee of Detail completes its report. The five members, Randolph, Wilson, Gorham, Ellsworth and Rutledge have worked hard to assemble the various resolutions into a single report. For form and structure, they refer to similar documents already in force, such as the Articles of Confederation and the various states constitutions. They do not consider that they are writing what will actually become the new Constitution, however, Bowen states. They methodically arrange the resolutions into sections.

At the meeting of August 6, Rutledge distributes a copy of the report to the state delegations, after which the meeting adjourns. Bowen imagines that although the report has nothing in it that is new to the delegates, seeing it all in one place must have been shocking to them. The delegations each meet to discuss the report, which can still be altered under the rules of the Convention.

The issue of slavery arises. Some delegates are staunchly against the practice on moral grounds and wish to see it abolished. Southern states rely on slave labor and will never support such a proposal. The middle ground is occupied by those who think that the national government should let states decide for themselves about slavery, assuming that the practice will eventually disappear.

A bargain is reached. Slaves will count at a ratio of five slaves to three free citizens for the purpose of determining representation in the House. In return, the slave trade is to be abolished after 1808. Slavery itself would still be legal. Bowen suggests that this is the second crucial compromise that saved the Convention and allowed the Constitution to see the light of day.

Foreigners in Congress. The Ten Miles Square. Summary and Analysis

Although the Convention seems to have made a huge stride in forming its final report, more and more questions arise as the summer heat wears on. The Convention takes up the matter of whether foreign-born citizens should be allowed to serve in Congress, and if so after how long a residence in the United States. As different residency requirements are discussed, it is pointed out that some would prevent current delegates from serving in Congress. This creates a paradox that a person might be considered eligible to form a new government, but not serve in it. After several votes, it is decided that foreigners may serve in the House after seven years' citizenship and in the Senate after nine years. The President will be required to be native born.

The question of where the new government should be located is another contentious issue. Congress at this time had moved from city to city, which is considered a disadvantage. Some states, such as New Jersey and Pennsylvania, would like to see the new government be installed in one of their cities. It is decided, however, that it should not be in a city that also houses a state government.

It is suggested by someone, Bowen says it is not known who exactly, that a new federal city be created that is ten miles square. This idea horrifies some of the delegates, who imagine a national fortress unimpeded by any law. This will also be used as an argument against ratification after the Constitution is referred to the states for approval. The final Constitution leaves the question to Congress as to where the federal district will be placed, indicating that it should not exceed ten miles square. The battle over the location will continue after ratification. It is discussed how often and when Congress should meet. The Convention decides on annual meetings to start in December.

Test Oaths, Deism and Tolerance. A Standing Army. Treason Defined. Summary and Analysis

The delegates grow weary of the constant re-examination of issues. A motion is passed that they will meet from 10 a.m. to 4 p.m. every day without adjourning any earlier. While they have agreed on the larger principles, they are mired in the details. As the Convention moves slowly toward finishing, members produce new ideas to be included.

The idea had been brought up earlier that the President and members of Congress should take an oath to uphold the Constitution. However, some delegates thought oaths unnecessary.

The question of a religious requirement arises. Most of the states have such a requirement, designed to keep all but protestant Christians from serving in high office. Many of the delegates and leading men of the day such as Jefferson, Franklin and John Adams are more accurately considered Deists, who claim belief in God, but do not adhere to a religious orthodoxy.

The Convention receives a letter from a leading citizen of Philadelphia, Jonas Phillips. Phillips is Jewish, and he writes about the current Pennsylvania Constitution, which requires a religious oath of office holders stating their belief in the Christian God. Philips, who is a veteran of the Revolutionary War, asks the Convention not to require any similar oath for service in the national government. In the end, the Constitution will prohibit any religious test as a qualification for public service.

Still working from the report of the Committee of Detail the Convention moves on to the question of a standing army. The idea is abhorrent to many delegates, who imagine a national army suppressing the states, or a military leader taking control of the country. No decision is made on this day, August 18.

On August 20, the subject of discussion is treason, and what should constitute it. Part of the question is whether an act against a state government would be treason against the United States. Each state has its own treason laws, which are sometimes stretched in whatever way necessary to punish or confiscate property from former Loyalists who supported Britain during the Revolution.

In the end, the Convention chooses to define treason narrowly as an act against the United States, and limits the punishment that Congress might inflict. The Constitution will also prohibit the punishment of the children of those convicted of treason by removing their right of inheritance.

It has now been three months since the Convention started. Bowen imagines that the delegates who support a strong Constitution such as Madison, Morris and Wilson may be feeling discouraged that the delegates still seem to be mired in small details and squabbling over the powers of the new government.

Who Shall Ratify? The People or the States? Summary and Analysis

It is August 30, and the end is in sight. Although no final adjournment date has been set, it is understood that they will not extend past September. Outside the State House, the states are becoming restless. A newspaper reports that states are neglecting the repair of their roads and canals awaiting the result of the Convention, in case a new national government will be taking responsibility for them.

An argument arises over how many states must agree to the proposed Constitution for it to be ratified. Numbers between seven and ten are considered, but some delegates, such as those from Maryland, believe that all 13 states should be required to ratify. Since Rhode Island has stayed away from the Convention and other delegates have left in protest, requiring 13 states to ratify will doom the new Constitution, Bowen suggests. With Maryland dissenting, it is voted that nine states will be required to ratify.

The question of how ratification should take place is considered. Some propose that state legislatures should decide. Some feel that there should be a popular vote. The supporters of a popular vote claim that state legislators, worried that they will lose power and influence under the new Constitution, will delay taking a vote on ratification. The Convention initially votes for popular ratification, but the question is not resolved for good. Once again, the matter of giving too much power to the common people is brought up as problematic.

The proposition is made that the states be allowed to propose amendments to the plan and return them for consideration at a second convention. After the long hot months spent hammering through the details of the present plan, some delegates despair that they have come so close to a finished document but now seem unable to clear the final hurdle. In the end, the Convention does not settle the ratification question. Bowen ends the chapter with a hint that the problem will be solved artfully by a committee.

Drafting the Constitution. The Committee of Style and Arrangement Take Hold. September 8-12. Summary and Analysis

Despite their deep differences, the Convention agrees to appoint a committee to assemble a final document that can be voted on by the whole. This committee consists of William Johnson, Alexander Hamilton, Governor Morris, James Madison and Rufus King. All five are supporters of a strong central government.

Bowen gives a brief summation of the qualities of each of these members, who would together write the core of the Constitution. Dr. Johnson is well liked by all the delegates, and is trusted in the South. He is the President of Columbia College in New York. Hamilton is recognized as an eloquent speaker and excellent writer, although his speech that leaned in favor of monarchy must worry some. Morris is known for his grasp of human nature, Bowen asserts, and Madison for his grasp of politics. King is widely respected.

The committee meets for four days. They strike on an expedient way to deal with the ratification debate by removing the articles concerning ratification and giving the responsibility to Congress in the form of two resolutions. This defuses one of the potentially explosive issues of the Convention.

Along with the draft of the new Constitution, the committee writes a letter to accompany the document to Congress to be signed by Washington. The letter leaves no doubt that the goal of the document is to "consolidate" the states into one nation.

The basis of the new national government is signaled in the proposed preamble, which begins with the now well-known words, "We the People..." This was a novel phrase at the time. Bowen states. The Confederacy drew its powers from the states, not directly from the people. This wording will draw fire from opponents during the ratification process.

Bowen steps into the present day and remarks on the legal terms that have come to surround the principles of the Constitution as it is discussed in modern law. The members of the committee could not have known how their words would be pored over for meaning and interpretation for the next two centuries, she imagines. In his papers after the fact, Bowen states that Madison gives Morris much of the credit for the wording of the final document. Afterward, some would challenge the language of the Constitution as ambiguous, yet others would praise it for its simplicity.

A Bill of Rights Rejected. Summary and Analysis

On September 12, with the Philadelphia newspapers reporting that an adjournment is near, the Committee of Style is ready to present the proposed constitution to the Convention. Bowen says that, as expected, the assembly proceeds to "tear the plan apart." (p. 243)

George Mason, concerned that the plan gives too much power to the government, raises the possibility of including a bill of rights to place limits on the government. This is the first time such a thing is mentioned by name at the Convention, Bowen states, although Charles Pinckney had made a similar proposal in August that was dropped.

Some delegates respond that the bills of rights that are already in effect in most states will still be valid, so one is not required for the Constitution. Mason replies that the new Constitution will have supreme power over the states, so one is necessary. By a vote of 10-0, however, the Convention decides not to include a bill of rights with the plan. Bowen remarks at this point that the Bill of Rights which would eventually be passed by the first Congress under the Constitution are so entwined with the Constitution itself that most Americans confuse them with the Constitution itself.

When the Constitution is published, the opponents to it make much of its lack of a bill of rights. Members of the Convention respond that the Constitution itself limits the government. When Gerry moves in the Convention to include a clause declaring a free press, it is argued that one is not necessary since Congress' power will not extend to the press. The motion fails.

Some delegates, such as Hamilton, even feel that bill of rights would be a dangerous precedent. Others argue that it is a futile gesture to attempt to name all the rights that men should enjoy, and that giving a suitable structure to the new government will itself result in the protection of citizens' rights.

Bowen omits giving any contemporary arguments in favor of a bill of rights, presuming that they are evident to the modern reader. She does include some contemporary thoughts on the matter from Thomas Jefferson, however, who writes to Washington about his astonishment that a bill of rights is not included. Jefferson states that this is one of two misgivings he has about the proposed Constitution, the other being no limit on the terms of the President. In newspapers everywhere, opinions on both sides of the question will be published.

Returning to the Convention, the assembly continues to make changes to the plan. The subject of apportionment returns as Delaware fights for more representatives in the first Congress. The question of how amendments will be made is debated.

Randolph stands to suggest that the plan be submitted to the states to offer changes and amendments, followed by a second Convention to consider an incorporate these proposals. George Mason seconds the motion. This is a crucial moment, Bowen states. Mason and Randolph are important delegates from Virginia, the most populous state. If they withdraw support from the plan, it may be doomed.

Charles Pinckney stands and states that he too has reservations about some of the finer points of the plan, but that to continue to submit it to changes will create confusion that will undo any good that any resulting plan might do. He resolves to support the plan. The delegates vote unanimously not to hold a second convention. They vote unanimously to approve the plan as amended, and then they adjourn.

The Constitution is Signed. The Dissidents. Summary and Analysis

On September 17, 40 delegates gather at the State House to approve the final version of the proposed Constitution. Benjamin Franklin produces a speech, which is read by Wilson. Franklin starts by stating that he does not entirely approve of the proposal. This is designed to get the attention of the members, and Bowen suggests that it does. Franklin continues, however, that he intends to support it despite his misgivings, because he recognizes that it is the best proposal that is possible. He urges the other members to put aside their hesitations and support the Constitution. He goes farther to suggest they not openly criticize the plan once it is made public.

Franklin moves that the Constitution be signed as approved by the states, and not by the individual members. This move, Bowen suggests, is strategic. It is designed to give the dissident delegates a chance to preserve their reservations while still signing. Before the question comes to a vote, however, Nathaniel Gorham stands to propose one final change. He asks that the clause that grants on representative for every 40,000 residents be changed to one of every 30,000. George Washington, presiding over the Convention, unexpectedly rises and gives a speech on the subject after months of virtual silence. Washington explains that he would like very much to see this change approved, and in deference to the General, the states vote for the change unanimously.

Randolph rises to speak, alluding to Franklin's speech. He says that despite Franklin's words, he himself cannot sign the Constitution. He states that he feels that it will fail to receive the ratification of the necessary nine states. Others express their intention not to sign.

This agitates Hamilton, who feels it crucial that all the delegates sign the final plan. Franklin speaks to say that he hopes Randolph will reconsider, as having such an important delegate absent from the signatures might harm the chances of success for any plan. Franklin's motion to sign the plan as coming from the states is voted on and passes.

George Mason remains silent thereafter, but writes his objections on his copy of the final plan. He will later send his list of objections to Washington. Mason also expresses his dismay that the Convention becomes impatient with the end in sight and passed over several key issues in a rush to finish.

The time comes to sign, and the delegates arrange themselves in geographic order. All the members present sign except Randolph and Mason of Virginia and Gerry of Massachusetts. The Convention adjourns, and the members retire to the City Tavern for a meal.

The Constitution Goes Before the Country. Summary and Analysis

With the business of the Convention completed, Bowen turns to the matter of ratification. This marks the fourth general section of the book.

As soon as copies are made available, newspapers across the land publish the proposed Constitution in its entirety. The reaction various, but all find it shocking, Bowen states. The first impression many have is that it is based on the British system in that it seemingly consolidates the independent states into an empire.

Supporters of the Constitution immediately begin publishing essays in several newspapers in favor of the new plan. The most noteworthy of these were written by Madison, Hamilton and John Jay and are signed anonymously as PUBLIUS. Collectively, these essays, which called for a strong national government, came to be known as the Federalist Papers.

An opposing group springs up, called Antifederalists. These opponents criticize Congress for acting so quickly to pass the question on to the states for ratification. The antifederalists include some of the well-known figures of the day such as Samuel Adams, Patrick Henry, George Mason and James Monroe.

The battle rages on in the state legislatures. In Pennsylvania, anti-Constitution forces try to stall action on appointing a convention for ratification, but fail. The ratification convention drags on for five weeks before finally approving of the Constitution. James Wilson, a vocal proponent of the Constitution, is beaten by a mob of anti-Constitution men.

Delaware is the first state to ratify, after it becomes clear that Pennsylvania will do so. New Jersey is next, Then Georgia. Connecticut follows, then Massachusetts. Virginia schedules its ratification convention for May. It will be one of the most contentious.

Massachusetts. The People Speak. Summary and Analysis

Bowen backs up and revisits the Massachusetts ratification convention. Massachusetts is considered mainly Antifederalist, being used to a town-meeting type of direct government that rejects delegated authority. The convention includes some of the men who had fought with Shays during the insurgence. They opposed the Constitution simply because the "wellborn" classes supported it, Bowen claims (p. 283).

The farmers from the rural parts of the state for the most part fear that the national government aims to take everything from them, including their property and freedom. They claim that the wealthier residents of the towns support the plan because they stand to gain positions in the new government.

Madison watches events unfold in Massachusetts carefully. In late January, he writes to Washington that things begin to be "very ominous" (p. 288). Massachusetts Governor John Hancock has stayed away from the convention, waiting for a majority to form before taking any action. Nothing can happen without him.

The idea arises to offer some conciliation to the antifederalists by including ten amendments as recommendations to Congress. Hancock presents this "conciliatory proposition" to the convention. For several days, the proposition is debated. Finally, the antifederalists give in and it is decided to send the proposed amendments to Congress along with the ratified Constitution. The vote is close. Bowen suggests that had Massachusetts failed to ratify, the Constitution would never have been ratified.

Virginia and New York. The Federal Procession. Summary and Analysis

Massachusetts is the sixth state to ratify. Maryland follows afterward, suggesting amendments of its own in the manner of Massachusetts. At the end of May, South Carolina ratifies, the eighth of the nine states needed to put the Constitution in force.

Virginia is largely antifederalist. Its convention closely examines each clause of the Constitution, tearing it apart. The antifederalists are led by the prominent Patrick Henry. Edmund Randolph, who introduced the Virginia Resolves at the Convention but eventually refused to sign the final plan, is the Governor of Virginia. He is widely thought to be an antifederalist, but Bowen says that since the Convention he has begun to change his thinking. When Randolph addresses the Virginia ratification convention, he offers a compromise based on the actions of Massachusetts and Maryland. He suggests that the convention offer a list of amendments along with the ratified constitution.

This idea is accepted, but the debate continues on whether Virginia should make its approval contingent on the adoption of the amendments, or if they should be recommended for adoption after the Constitution goes into effect. Patrick Henry attacks Randolph for his apparent about face on the issue. Henry also ridicules the idea of merely making suggestions for amendments to be made after adoption. He threatens to leave the convention should such a decision be made.

Henry's opponents accuse him of threatening to secede from the Union, which Henry denies. In the end, the Virginia convention ratifies the Constitution and returns it to congress with a list of twenty resolutions and twenty amendments for Congress to consider following adoption. Antifederalists raise a protest outside the convention, but Henry dispels them, telling them there duty is to support to Union.

In New York, the strong antifederalist faction is disappointed by Virginia's ratification. Bowen states that the debates in New York are the same as in the other states, and does not elaborate on them. The margin in New York is only three votes in favor of ratification. Like other states, the New York convention includes a list of proposed amendments.

Eventually all 13 states will ratify the Constitution. As soon as the required nine states have ratified, the states begin to organize grand celebrations of the event. Ships are mounted on wagons and pulled through the streets along with parades of soldiers and craftsmen, all proclaiming the glory of the new nation.

Important People

General George Washington

Bowen opens the narrative with the arrival of George Washington in Philadelphia to attend the Convention as a representative from Virginia. Washington is one of the most prominent and celebrated people of the day. When he arrives, he is welcomed openly and publicly by the people of Philadelphia.

Washington lives at Mount Vernon in Virginia on a large farm. He takes a personal interest in the farming operations, during his time in Philadelphia writes specific instructions to his farm managers, and inquires about what is happening. In the short breaks in the meeting, he spends part of his time riding around the farmlands around Philadelphia learning about local crops and cultivation techniques.

In deference to his status, Washington is made President of the Convention, and Bowen states that it is understood that whatever the new form of government that results, Washington will be at the head of it. Despite his prominence, Washington is nearly silent during the convention. His one speech, Bowen relates, is very near the end as the Convention prepares to vote on a final plan.

Washington is a dignified man in his 50s, one of the older delegates and certainly one of the most respected. Not everyone of the day agrees that Washington is as infallible as he is sometimes portrayed, but Bowen asserts that nobody questions his dignity and integrity.

James Madison

James Madison is a delegate from Virginia and is perhaps the most adept political theorist among the delegates. He keeps the most detailed notes of the proceedings of the Convention, spending most of his time between sessions filling out his notes. Madison is in his mid 30s. He is a Congressman representing Virginia as well, and arrives in Philadelphia from New York, where Congress is in session.

Madison's account of the Convention provides most of the material for Bowen's narrative. He shows himself to be a very thorough writer and thinker through his detailed account. Bowen remarks on the fact that while many delegates arrive days and weeks after the Convention begins, Madison arrives several days early. This is indicative of his wish to be well prepared for every task. In consultation with Thomas Jefferson, Madison has already studied the forms and histories of many governments from around the world, and has outlined the features he wishes to see in the new government.

Madison is a small man, and speaks very quietly. Although not physically imposing, he is intellectually a giant, and is one of the leading fighters for the Constitution during the fight for ratification. His work in Virginia was crucial, matching words with the formidable Patrick Henry, who opposed ratification.

Along with Alexander Hamilton and John Jay, Madison penned the anonymous Federalist Papers, a group of essays in favor of the new Constitution, which are some of the most influential writings in American history. Madison would become the fourth US President.

Alexander Hamilton

Hamilton is a young lawyer representing New York at the Convention. During the Revolutionary War, he served as an aide to General Washington, who admires and respects him. Hamilton's character is quite different from Washington's, however. He is brash and impatient. He is in his early 30s at the time of the Convention.

Hamilton is out of step with the other two delegates from New York, who never vote the same way as he. Indeed, he is somewhat out of step with the entire Convention, as evidenced by his six-hour speech advocating a hereditary leader for America who is chosen for life. This, along with Hamilton's foreign-born mannerisms and speech, lead many to assume him to be calling for an American monarch, which, Bowen explains, he probably was.

Hamilton eventually leaves the Convention, perhaps embarrassed by his speech. He returns after a time, however, and is the only delegate from New York to sign the final plan, the other two delegates having left in protest.

Hamilton joins with Madison and John Jay to write the Federalist Papers, and becomes one of the strongest proponents for the Constitution during ratification. He would be named the first Secretary of the Treasury by President Washington.

Benjamin Franklin

Benjamin Franklin is a nearly legendary figure in American history, and by Bowen's account, he was already a near legend at the time of the Convention. Franklin is an old man in his 80s and is in poor health. Unable to walk, he is carried each day to the State House in a sedan chair brought from Europe and carried by prisoners. He is the President of Pennsylvania. Franklin lives in a house near the State House and regularly receives visits from delegates.

Franklin takes on the role of the wise old man of the Convention, offering calming words when tempers run high. His age prevents him from standing and making speeches in a bold voice, but he does produce speeches that he asks others to read for him. The delegates defer to Franklin, seconding his motions even when they have no chance of passing.

Franklin has traveled widely in Europe and has served as a diplomat for the American states. In France, he is celebrated as a great thinker and admired for his charm.

New Hampshire Delegates

The New Hampshire delegates arrive several weeks after the Convention begins, at the height of the debate between the large and small states. The members are John Langdon and Nicholas Gilman.

Massachusetts Delegates

Massachusetts, while not the largest state, is nonetheless influential as the birthplace of the Revolution. Its delegates are Gerry, Gorham, King and Strong. Elbridge Gerry is one of the few delegates who refuses to sign the final plan. Gerry publishes open protests to the proposed Constitution during the ratification battle. Nathanial Gorham serves as the chairman of the Committee of the Whole Rufus King is one of the five delegates assigned to write the final draft of the plan. King is a well respected member of Congress.

Connecticut Delegates

The Connecticut delegates are: Johnson, Sherman and Ellsworth. William Samuel Johnson is the president of Columbia College and a well-respected doctor. Roger Sherman is a vocal member of the Convention opposed to the inclusion of a bill of rights. Sherman is the first to suggest equal representation in the Senate and proportional representation in the House, but his idea is not taken up at the time.

New York Delegates

The New York delegates are Robert Yates, John Lansing, Jr. and Alexander Hamilton. All three leave the Convention early. Yates and Lansing leave in protest of the national government that is favored by the Convention. They do not return. Hamilton does return, and is the only delegate from New York to sign the final plan.

New Jersey Delegates

The New Jersey delegates are: Paterson, Brearly, Houston, Livingston and Dayton. William Paterson, early on, proposes a federal form of government as an alternate to the national form proposed by Virginia. Paterson leaves the Convention before it has finished, returning to his New Jersey law practice.

Pennsylvania Delegates

Pennsylvania sends one of the largest delegations, and is one of the larger states. Delegates include: Mifflin, Morris, clymer, Ingersoll, Fitzsimmons, Wilson, Morris and Franklin. Robert Morris is the wealthy Philadelphian who hosted General Washington during the Convention. James Wilson is one of the more frequent speakers in the Convention who proposes the three-fifths rule. Wilson makes the motion that the Executive branch be led by a single President. Governor Morris is one of the Committee of Style and Arrangement who drafts the final Constitution. Madison gives Morris most of the credit for the final style and arrangement of the document.

Delaware Delegates

Delaware's delegates are: Read, Bedford, Dickinson, Bassett and Broom. Gunning Bedford supports the New Jersey federal plan. John Dickinson, a well known author and vocal proponent of a national government, is chair of the committee that drafts the Articles of Confederation.

Maryland Delegates

The Maryland delegates are: McHenry, Daniel of St. Thomas Jenifer, Carroll, Mercer and Martin. Luther Martin, noted for his long-winded speeches, leaves the Convention two weeks before it is signed.

Virginia Delegates

The Virginia Delegates include: Washington, Randolph, Blair, Madison, Jr., Mason, Wythe and McClurg. George Washington is President of the Convention. Edmund Randolph is the Governor of Virginia who presents the Virginia Resolves upon which the final plan will be based. He refuses to sign the final plan and publishes essays opposing it during ratification. Randolph eventually supports ratification with a bill of rights. George Mason, author of the Virginia bill of rights and a proponent of including a bill of rights in the Constitution, refuses to sign the final plan.

Georgia Delegates

The Georgia delegates are: Few, Baldwin, Pierce and Houstoun.

North Carolina Delegates

The North Carolina delegates are: Martin, Richardson Davie, Dobbs Spaight, Blount and Williamson.

South Carolina Delegates

The South Carolina delegates are: Rutledge, Pinckney, Cotesworth

Pinckney and Butler.

Objects/Places

Philadelphia*appears in* non-fiction

Philadelphia is the capital of Pennsylvania situated along the Delaware River. Philadelphia is a small bustling city at the time of the Convention, with a busy port and regular market.

Pennsylvania State House*appears in* non-fiction

Located in Philadelphia, the Pennsylvania State House is now called Independence Hall. It was the location of the signing of the Declaration of independence and the Articles of Confederation, and the seat of the Second Continental Congress during the Revolutionary War. It is the location of the Constitutional Convention.

Articles of Confederation*appears in* non-fiction

The Articles of Confederation is the document by which the thirteen American states agree to a common, federal government. While the articles spell out the nature of this agreement, they do not provide the federal government with any power to regulate interstate commerce or to collect taxes. As a result, states come up with their own exclusionary trade rules and refuse to pay their share of the expenses from the Revolutionary War. The Convention in Philadelphia is called to consider revising the Articles of Confederation to address these problems.

Congress*appears in* non-fiction

Congress at this time is the single body designated by the Articles of Confederation made up of representatives from each state. The Articles provide for no national capital, and so Congress has moved from place to place. It is by an act of Congress that the Convention has been called, and many of the delegates to the Convention are also members of Congress.

The Virginia Resolves*appears in* non-fiction

The Virginia Resolves is a plan presented by Edmund Randolph of Virginia forming a national government that is separate from and superior to the state governments. The plan provides a road map for the delegates to consider many of the important issues related to the new government. Its provisions are debated, adopted, amended and rejected repeatedly over the course of the Convention. By the end, Randolph will refuse to even sign the final plan. Nevertheless, many of the basic principles proposed in the Virginia Resolves find their way into the United States Constitution.

The New Jersey Plan*appears in* non-fiction

The New Jersey Plan of government is presented by Paterson of New Jersey. It calls for a federal government and preserves the sovereignty of the individual states. It stands in contrast to the Virginia Plan which calls for a supreme national government. The Convention votes to proceed along the lines of the Virginia plan.

The Great Compromise*appears in* non-fiction

The Great Compromise is reached by the Convention concerning the representation of the states in the legislative branch. The Great

Compromise allowed for proportional representation in the House of Representatives based on population and equal representation in the Senate, with each state receiving two votes. This balanced the concerns of the large and small states.

The Western Territory*appears in* non-fiction

The Western Territory is the unincorporated territory of America that stretched from the Appalachian Mountains in the east to the eastern bank of the Mississippi River in the west, and from the Great Lakes in the north to Spanish Florida in the south. This area was closed to settlement during British rule, but was opened again after independence. Settlers and land speculators began streaming into the region, to the concern of many in government. The Western Territory is an important matter to the Convention, which must determine how new states will be allowed into the Union, and on what level of participation in the government.

Rhode Island*appears in* non-fiction

Rhode Island is the smallest of the thirteen states, and the only state not to send delegates to the Convention.

Spanish Louisiana and Spanish Florida*appears in* non-fiction

Spanish Louisiana and Florida are regions to the west and south of the Western Territory. Spain also claims a portion of the southernmost portion of the Western Territory, and navigation on the Mississippi River. Some delegates fear that if settlers in the Western Territory are alienated by the new Constitution, they may take sides with Spain.

Themes

The human aspects of the Convention and delegates

Any author taking on the narrative of such a momentous historical event as the Constitutional Convention must address the myths and legends that have arisen around the event over time. The founding fathers hold such an elevated place in American history that it is sometimes difficult to imagine them as living, breathing people. This is what Bowen aims to do in her narrative, and she includes several small details to bring the Convention into the everyday world familiar to her readers.

One of the thematic details that Bowen focuses on is the weather. In nearly every chapter, she refers to the oppressive heat of the Philadelphia summer. She adds a description of the woolen clothing common in the day to paint a vivid description of discomfort. By including such details, Bowen enriches the scene without detracting from the importance of the events. If anything, the growing physical discomfort experienced by the delegates adds to the glory of the events when viewed from centuries afterwards.

Bowen also relies heavily on the sometimes personal remarks left behind by the delegates in their journals and letters. These remarks express the doubts and pessimism that some of America's founding fathers felt at the dawn of the new country. Some of their opinions seem startling today, such as Hamilton's proposal that the President be appointed for life, and that the position be hereditary. These additions show the founding fathers so often portrayed as giants of patriotism and political thought to be fallible human beings with a wide range of views.

While Bowen aims to show the Convention delegates as humans with real human aspects, she stops short of showing all their probable faults.

For instance, she mentions that many of the delegates stood to lose or gain personally based on the outcome of the Convention. She suggest, perhaps a little weakly, that while they all were aware that the new national government could affect their financial and political fortunes they were able to put these aside and act in the interest of the Union.

The role of the Convention in the eyes of the delegates

The official task of the Convention in Philadelphia is to consider revisions to the Articles of Confederation that currently govern the thirteen states. What they produce is a completely new national government, far exceeding their mandate.

Nearly from the beginning, as soon as Randolph presents the Virginia Resolves, which will frame the debate for the rest of the summer, it becomes clear to the delegates that they are considering nothing less than a completely new government that is separate from and superior to the state governments. Those delegates who are concerned about this loss of state powers object on the grounds that the Convention is not authorized to make such wide-sweeping changes.

As the Convention moves steadily toward proposing a national government, these objections transition into claims that such a plan will not gain acceptance among the states or their citizens. Time and again, Bowen relates, the delegates stop to consider how their proposals will appear to the public once they are made known. Even in the final days of the Convention, after the majority have approved of the new Constitution, there are those who refuse to sign it claiming that it will never be ratified by the necessary nine states.

Bowen revisits these concerns throughout the narrative. She includes the viewpoints of those outside as well as inside the secret proceedings to provide a balance between the two. Bowen describes the delegates as trying to maintain practical outlooks on their actions, aiming to balance the reforms they feel are needed with what they feel the public will actually accept. She takes the Convention out of the academic world of political theory, and places it in the practical world of human society.

The modern reader already knows the role these men played in history.

Bowen expresses repeatedly, by showing the many ways in which they themselves are unsure of what they should do, or if what they proposed will be accepted, how the delegates are very much a part of their society.

Divisions between the states

As Bowen points out, ever since the Civil War, Americans have become used to thinking of division between the states as between North and South. While this division is present among the original 13 states, other perhaps deeper divisions run between the states at the time of the Constitutional Convention. Bowen reveals these in the course of her narrative and explains how they lead to the Constitution's final form. The potential for disunion between the states is, Bowen suggests, one of the biggest reasons for calling the Convention into being, the Articles of Confederation not being sufficient to keep them together.

The primary division between the states is between the large and small. Virginia is the most populous state, and has the strongest presence at the Convention, with men like George Washington, James Madison and George Mason representing it. It is the plan brought by the Virginia delegation that first suggests a strong national government, and which serves as the basis for most of the final plan the Convention agrees upon. At the other end of the spectrum is tiny Rhode Island, which has declined to send any delegates at all to the Convention, wanting no part of what its leaders feel will only result in the large states gaining power over the small.

This division in size is a crucial consideration in the long battle over how the states will be represented in Congress. Several proposals are made. The larger states favor a system based only on population, which will give them an advantage. The smaller states in general wish for equal representation, with each state having an equal vote. This division threatens to dissolve the entire undertaking but is averted by what is now called the Great Compromise. This compromise provides for proportional representation in the House of Representative, but equal representation in the Senate.

The division between North and South is also part of the representation issue, as the question of slavery arises. The delegates must decide if slaves count as inhabitants for the purposes of apportioning representation in the House. It is decided that for this purpose, slaves will be counted at a ratio of three-fifths.

As deep as these divisions run, Bowen speculates that the Convention and the ensuing Constitution actually prevent what might become an even deeper problem between the East and West. The Western Territory, closed during British rule, is now open to settlement in many places. The more sophisticated residents of the Atlantic cities look on these settlers as "uncouth" and inexperienced in the important matter of government. There is a strong feeling among some of the delegates that any new states formed from this territory should not be admitted to the United States on an equal footing with the Atlantic states. Already, settlers in some frontier regions are threatening to form their own states, making the matter urgent.

Other delegates insist that new states must be allowed to enter as equals of existing states. Some reason that it is unlikely that the western states would ever outnumber the eastern states. Others point out the similarity between the present situation and the situation that prevailed while the states were under British rule. Keeping the western states inferior to the eastern might lead to rebellion and war. With Britain and Spain holding territory on the frontier borders, this possibility seems even more dangerous as rebellious states may seek assistance from those countries, which would be only too happy to help weaken the new country.

In the end, the compromise and negotiation that Bowen outlines in her narrative overcome these real and potential divisions between the states, leading to a real Union.

Style

Perspective

Bowen tells the story of the Constitutional Convention largely through the eyes of the delegates involved. Quoting extensively from the notes and letters of the actual delegates, she gives an inside look at the Convention, whose proceedings were secret at the time they were held.

The official minutes of the meetings are spare an businesslike, Bowen says, but many of the delegates keep more personal accounts of the discussions, giving insight into the motivations and opinions of the individuals involved. James Madison keeps extensive notes, using all his spare time between meetings to flesh them out. Bowen relies mainly on Madison's account, supplemented by those of others. This raises the possibility that there may be differing accounts of the same discussions, but if any vary significantly, Bowen does not say. In this way, the perspective on the events is perhaps somewhat slanted, as Bowen may have made decisions on which account to follow without indicating whether other versions exist.

Bowen mines the letters the delegates write home to their families from Philadelphia for personal information. In the letters of Washington, for instance, the General's weariness at the constant argument among the delegations is revealed. Letters written after the Convention, which Bowen occasionally inserts during the events they refer to, reveal the key turning points of the meeting and the major issues that threatened to dissolve it.

Bowen also includes perspectives from outside the State Hall where the secret Convention is being held. She includes excerpts from contemporary newspaper clippings that speculate on the business inside, as well as letters between important Americans who are not members of the Convention, such as John Adams and Thomas

Jefferson.

She finds an outside perspective on the new country and its people as a whole in the writings of foreign visitors to America, who send letters and publish books on the unusual people they find in the United States. These perspectives point out how different America is from Europe at this time.

As a whole, the perspective of the narrative is from the point of view of someone familiar with American history who already knows the outcome of the events described, and much of the background of the people involved. Bowen takes advantage of this presumed familiarity to streamline her narrative. She need not fully introduce George Washington before mentioning his arrival in Philadelphia, or go into detail about the life of Benjamin Franklin.

Tone

The tone of Bowen's narrative is reverential and celebratory, but also realistic. Her aim seems to be to elucidate the events and give them a human touch rather than to simply spell out the events as they happen and analyze the proceedings. She picks out details about the men whose names are well known to most Americans to provide them with more human characteristics. Benjamin Franklin is carried in a sedan chair to the Convention each day. Alexander Hamilton is something of a hotheaded youth. George Washington barely speaks, merely smiling or frowning at the topic at hand.

Bowen includes these human characteristics, but never denigrates or judges the people she describes. Bowen suggests that many of the delegates stood to gain personally both politically and financially based on the form of the new Constitution, but stops short of accusing any of them of acting out of personal interest. To do so would be counter to the essentially reverential tone of the narrative. Even characters who may be genuinely corrupt, such as the land speculator Mannaseh Cutler, are merely outlined.

Bowen also brings the events of the story into the real world by including frequent descriptions of the hot weather and the stifling State

House, which is shut up to prevent eavesdroppers from listening to the secret proceedings at the windows. This adds another human element, and adds to the adversity that must be overcome by the delegates. This in turn supports the celebratory tone once the seemingly impossible has been achieved.

Structure

The book is presented in 25 relatively short chapters. There are no formal section divisions, but the narrative is divided into four thematic sections. The first half of the book gives a roughly chronological account of the origins and first months of the Convention. Because the delegates continually visit and revisit various issues, this chronological approach has its limitations, as something decided one day might be reversed or amended a few days, weeks or months later. Bowen has to move back and forth in time while following the timeline to account for these changes, making the chronological approach problematic at times.

About half way through the narrative, Bowen inserts two chapters describing the physical features of the new United States and the American people. For these descriptions, Bowen relies heavily on the contemporary accounts of foreign visitors. These accounts give an "outsider" view of the country, and reinforce the unique nature of the country and the new government it is trying to implement.

As part of the physical description of America at the time, Bowen describes the Western Territory, providing a transition into the third section of the book, which focuses on some of the main issues the Convention is considering. The Western Territory and the subject of new states formed from it are two of the issues that become contentious as the Convention enters its final weeks. The third section also highlights some of the divisions that have arisen among the delegates. Bowen uses these differences to build tension in the narrative as the close of the convention nears. With the end in sight, the Convention is in danger of breaking up. Through compromise and negotiation, a final Constitution is proposed, ending the third section of the book. The fourth portion of the narrative follows the battle for ratification, when many of the issues brought up in the Convention are fought out in the open within the states. Finally, Bowen includes the text of the Constitution in an appendix.

Bowen writes in a narrative style free from footnotes and citations, apart from a few notes at the end of the book. This lends fluidity to the narrative that makes for a more readable book than a more academic approach would have produced. However, it does require the author to include much of the background information in the main body of the text, producing many digressions and breaks in the narrative that can distract the reader.

Quotes

"The truth was that Franklin's character had always been puzzling. America was proud of the Doctor, proud that he had 'tamed the lightning' and that he was everywhere received as a citizen of the world. Yet a citizen of the world is inevitably suspect at home." - Chapter II, p. 17

"On May thirtieth, debate in the Convention opened by Randolph's suggesting an amended version of his first three resolves. Plainly, the Virginia members had been at work out-of-doors. A union of the states 'merely federal,' said Randolph, would not accomplish the object for which they were met. He therefore proposed ' a national government, consisting of a supreme legislative, executive and judicial.' Silence followed, complete and ominous." Chapter IV, p. 41

"The Convention of '87 discussed America not in terms of social philosophy but in relation to the country as they saw it around them. In the fields were no wretched peasant tenants, subsisting by their lord's favor. These men owned the land they cultivated." Chapter VI, p. 72

"It was closing time. members went out into the afternoon heat, walking wearily through the streets to lodgings which afforded little relief. In Dr. Franklin's garden the mulberry tree gave hospitable shade. Yet on days like this, if a breeze stirred it was from the southwest, a breath from the furnace. The city sweltered and the delegates endured." Chapter VIII, p. 96

"Alexander Hamilton at the Federal Convention cuts a disappointing figure, at odds with his previous and subsequent magnificent performance in support of the the Constitution. His long speech - a day's work - was out of tune, unacceptable to both sides." Chapter IX, p. 114

"Delegates had already voted against equality of representation in the House. After more than two weeks of debate the Convention voted again - and could not break the deadlock. The large states stood firm, though Madison had a way of placing the blame for obduracy always on the small states." Chapter XI, p. 128

"The bragging and the boasting were in truth part of a young vigor, a young defiance. America must shout aloud her name, her independence. All the world must be informed of her grandiose new plans, which encompassed a continent and concerned nothing less than the equality of men. 'We are making experiments,' Franklin had said." Chapter XIII, p. 165

"Not the least surprising characteristic of the Federal Convention was that, contrary to the tradition of political assemblies, it let itself be swayed by men of thought and historical perspective." Chapter XIV, p. 179

"No fewer than sixty ballots were needed before the method of selecting the President was decided; repeatedly, delegates fell upon it as if never before debated." Chapter XV, p. 189

"Most of the states included a religious qualification in their oaths for officeholders; many of these discriminated against Catholics, Jews, Deists and unbelievers. Beyond the cardinal principle that church and state must be separate, religion in America was a matter for local option and had been since the beginning." Chapter XVIII, p. 215

"Newspapers everywhere published the Constitution as soon as they could lay hands on it. So many columns had never been given over to a political subject in America. Correspondents wrote in, angry, approving or frightened as the case might be. The country was shocked, startled." Chapter XXIII, p. 267

"As soon as a majority of nine was assured, state by state held joyful celebration, animosity for the moment forgotten. Perhaps this is endemic to America; once the vote is counted, everybody wants to be in the parade." Chapter XXV, p. 306

Topics for Discussion

Bowen uses the word "Miracle" in the title of the book. What is miraculous about the events she describes?

The thirteen states still consider themselves almost as independent countries in alliance with one another. How is this idea of state sovereignty addressed in the final plan of the Constitution? Is it preserved or destroyed?

Discuss the political and geographic differences between the states that lead to division during the Convention.

How does Bowen's characterization of Washington, Madison, Hamilton and Franklin compare with the more common images of these men in American history?

Bowen does not give citations or use footnotes in the narrative, even when quoting directly from primary sources. How does this technique affect the reading of the book?

Bowen focuses her narrative on a very specific timeframe. What are the advantages and disadvantages to this approach of writing history?

What are some of the obstacles historians face when writing about people and events that are already well-known? How does Bowen address these obstacles?

www.ingramcontent.com/pod-product-compliance
Ingram Content Group UK Ltd.
Pitfield, Milton Keynes, MK11 3LW, UK
UKHW041920190726
13854UKWH00003B/1355

9 781304 556653